EXPLORE
WEATHER
~ AND ~
CLIMATE!

Kathleen M. Reilly

Illustrated by Bryan Stone

D0813869

green press INITIATIVE

Nomad Press is committed to preserving ancient forests and natural resources.
We elected to print *Explore Weather and Climate!* on 30% post consumer recycled paper,
processed chlorine free. As a result, for this printing, we have saved:

10 Trees (40' tall and 6-8" diameter)
4,526 Gallons of Wastewater
4 million BTU's of Total Energy
286 Pounds of Solid Waste
1,004 Pounds of Greenhouse Gases

Nomad Press made this paper choice because our printer, Thomson-Shore, Inc., is a member of
Green Press Initiative, a nonprofit program dedicated to supporting authors, publishers,
and suppliers in their efforts to reduce their use of fiber obtained from endangered forests.

For more information, visit www.greenpressinitiative.org

Nomad Press
A division of Nomad Communications
10 9 8 7 6 5 4 3 2 1

Copyright © 2011 by Nomad Press. All rights reserved.
No part of this book may be reproduced in any form without permission in writing from
the publisher, except by a reviewer who may quote brief passages in a review or **for limited educational use**.
The trademark "Nomad Press" and the Nomad Press logo are trademarks of Nomad Communications, Inc.

This book was manufactured by Thomson-Shore, Inc.,
Dexter, Michigan, USA
January 2012, Job #578504
ISBN: 978-1-936313-84-6

Illustrations by Bryan Stone
Educational Consultant, Marla Conn

Questions regarding the ordering of this book should be addressed to
Independent Publishers Group
814 N. Franklin St.
Chicago, IL 60610
www.ipgbook.com

Nomad Press
2456 Christian St.
White River Junction, VT 05001
www.nomadpress.net

Manufactured by Thomson-Shore, Dexter, MI (USA); RMA578RC504, December, 2011

MIX
Paper from
responsible sources
FSC® C013483

CONTENTS

Titles in the **Explore Your World!** Series

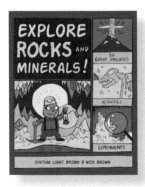

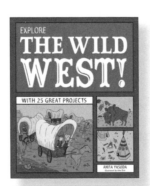

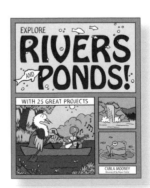

INTRODUCTION

WORDS TO KNOW

weather: what it's like outside—warm, cold, sunny, cloudy, rainy, snowy, or windy.

temperature: how warm or cold something is.

Have you ever played outside in the sunshine, flown a kite, or made a snowman? If so, you already know something about **weather**. As soon as you step outside, you feel the **temperature** on your skin and the wind in your hair. Or maybe you feel raindrops or snowflakes landing on your head!

That's the great thing about our planet—there are all different kinds of weather to enjoy. But weather can also mess up your plans. It can rain when you want to ride your bike, or be too cold when you want to swim.

1

When you think about it, weather is pretty amazing. Why does it snow one day and rain the next? What makes the wind? And why is there thunder and lightning?

WORDS TO KNOW

- **tornado:** a violent, twisting column of air.

- **hurricane:** a bad storm with high winds.

- **flood:** when water covers an area that is usually dry.

- **weather pattern:** repeating weather over a number of days or weeks.

- **weather forecast:** to say what the weather will be.

- **predict:** to say what will happen in the future.

- **weather instrument:** a tool that measures wind, temperature, or something else about the weather.

- **climate:** the average weather in an area over a long period of time.

The power of weather is amazing too. **Tornadoes** and **hurricanes** can completely demolish trees and houses. **Floods** can sweep away everything in their path. And freezing rain can knock down electric power lines and plunge thousands of people into darkness.

In this book you'll explore all these things—and more. You'll learn why some areas have different **weather patterns** than others, and how **weather forecasts** can **predict** the weather. You'll discover what makes snow, rain, and sleet, and just what clouds and rainbows are all about. And you'll learn how to build your own **weather instruments**, teach your family and friends how to stay safe from extreme weather, and even eat some clouds!

So, turn the page and let's start exploring weather and **climate**!

WHAT'S THE WEATHER?

Imagine it's Saturday morning. You wake up and get dressed to go outside. You pull on some shorts and a T-shirt and run out the door into—knee-deep snow. Oops! You didn't think about what the weather was going to be like.

Of course, it's unusual for there to be snow when you think it's going to be warm. But weather can change dramatically sometimes. Even within seasons, big changes in the weather can affect your outdoor plans. Think about summer. You might picture it as always sunny and hot. But it can certainly rain during summer. Or it can even be chilly. Sometimes severe weather—like a thunderstorm—can rattle calm summer afternoons.

3

Weather affects our lives every day and can change our plans. If it's snowy or icy, school might be closed. A rainy day might cancel your trip to the beach. And if there's hazardous weather coming, with the threat of strong thunderstorms or tornadoes, you need to stay alert and get to a safe place. That's why people are always wondering when they get up, "What's the weather going to be like today?"

THE WEATHER MAN

Have you ever turned on the TV or radio and heard someone telling you what the weather will be for the week? People who study the weather are called **meteorologists**. They **observe** the movement of **air masses**, changing temperatures, and **air pressure** to predict what the weather will be like in an hour, tomorrow, or next week. It's not an exact science. Sometimes forecasters will say it's going to rain buckets, and you only end up with a drizzle!

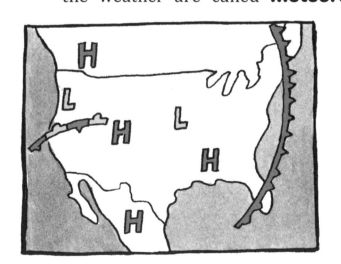

WORDS TO KNOW

meteorologist: a person who studies the science of weather and climate.

observe: to look at things carefully.

air mass: a large pocket of air that is different from the air around it.

air pressure: the force of the gases surrounding the earth pressing downward (sometimes called barometric pressure).

WHAT'S THE WEATHER?

WORDS TO KNOW

prediction: something you predict.

barometer: a weather instrument that measures air pressure.

anemometer: a weather instrument that measures wind speed.

observation: something you observe.

weather satellite: a small electronic object that circles the earth and sends back pictures of weather patterns.

radar: a system that sends out pulses of radio waves that reflect back.

Accurate weather **predictions** are important for planning. Farmers need to know when to plant their crops. Airlines need to know if it will be safe to fly. But there are so many things that go into figuring out what the weather is going to be that even meteorologists can get it wrong.

HOW FORECASTERS MAKE PREDICTIONS

Weather forecasters use computers to show a specific picture of what's going on with the weather. But the computers don't tell them everything. It's up to meteorologists to also make **observations** and understand weather trends and patterns. This helps them understand what the computer is showing them. They also use **weather satellites** and Doppler **radar** to spot weather that's on the way.

DID YOU KNOW?
Before computers, weather forecasters predicted the weather using mechanical instruments like **barometers** and **anemometers** and by looking outside.

5

Normal radar works by sending out a signal that bounces off an object and returns. It shows that something is there—but it's often hard to know what that something is. Doppler radar also sends out a signal that returns, but it can measure wind speed, type of **precipitation**, and even hail size. Doppler radar can also tell meteorologists whether an object is coming or going.

WORDS TO KNOW

precipitation: water in the air in any form, like snow, hail, or rain, that falls to the ground.

technology: tools, methods, and systems used to solve a problem or do work.

atmosphere: the gases surrounding the earth.

Forecasts are not always perfect, but as **technology** improves they are more and more accurate all the time. Today, forecasts are usually accurate up to about five days in advance. Some of the things weather forecasters try to predict include:

TEMPERATURE: The sun heats the earth and the **atmosphere**. This makes you feel warm. Of course, if the sun's not shining down because of thick cloud cover, you're going to feel colder.

PRECIPITATION: Everyone wants to know, "Is it going to rain today?" But rain isn't the only kind of precipitation. Precipitation is any form of moisture that falls to the earth's surface, including snow, sleet, freezing rain, and hail.

WHAT'S THE WEATHER?

AIR PRESSURE: Also called **barometric pressure**, this is the force of Earth's atmosphere pushing down. Air might be invisible, but it has weight. Cold air is **dense**, so it sinks. This is because the **molecules** in air are packed together when it's cold. Warm air is lighter, so it rises. Strong winds occur when the air pressure changes.

WORDS TO KNOW

- **barometric pressure:** the force of the atmosphere pressing downward (also called air pressure).

- **dense:** when molecules are pressed tightly together.

- **molecule:** a group of the tiniest particles.

LOOKS LIKE NICE WEATHER!

Before there were any weather instruments, people simply observed nature to predict the weather. Some of these observations turned out to be quite accurate, too! People even made sayings to help them remember the predictions.

"DEW ON THE GRASS, NO RAIN WILL PASS"

If it didn't rain overnight, check the grass in the morning. If it's dry, that means strong breezes have already dried the dew. Strong breezes often mean rain. If the grass is still wet with dew, there's no wind and it probably won't rain.

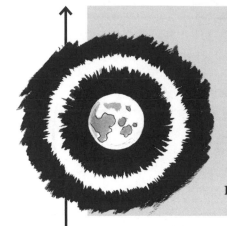

"HALO AROUND THE MOON OR SUN, RAIN IS COMING ON THE RUN"

A ring around the sun or moon is created by light passing through ice crystals at high **altitude**. When moisture is that high, it means an active weather system bringing rain or snow is heading your way quickly.

"WHEN LEAVES SHOW THEIR UNDERSIDES, BE VERY SURE THAT RAIN BETIDES" ('BETIDES' MEANS 'WILL HAPPEN')

Humidity can soften some leaves, making them curl or turn over. Humidity indicates that rain could be on the way. But this saying only works for certain kinds of trees, such as oak and poplar.

WORDS TO KNOW

altitude: the height of something above the level of the sea. Also called elevation.

humidity: a high amount of moisture in the air.

"WHEN THE WIND IS FROM THE EAST, 'TIS NEITHER GOOD FOR MAN NOR BEAST"

The wind is a great indicator of weather. To find out which way the wind is blowing, toss a piece of grass in the air. If the wind is from the east, it means rain is coming. If it's very strong from the east, a storm is coming.

8

WHAT'S THE WEATHER?

"A COW WITH HER TAIL TO THE WEST MAKES WEATHER BEST"

A cow stands with its back to the wind so it can smell animals sneaking around that might want to eat it. So, if a cow is standing with its tail to the west, that means the wind is coming from the west. And that means nice weather.

"RED SKY AT NIGHT, SAILOR'S DELIGHT; RED SKY AT MORNING, SAILORS TAKE WARNING"

Remember that the sun rises in the east and sets in the west. But weather patterns travel from west to east in the **Northern Hemisphere**.

Red skies are caused by sunlight reflecting off clouds. If the sky is red in the evening, that means the clouds are moving away eastwards, leaving clear skies behind. But if the sky is a deep red in the morning, that means moist clouds are coming in from the west, bringing rain.

WORDS TO KNOW

Northern Hemisphere: the half of the earth north of the **equator**. The southern half is called the Southern Hemisphere.

equator: an invisible line dividing the earth into the Northern and Southern Hemispheres.

"CRICKETS CAN TELL THE TEMPERATURE"

If you hear a cricket chirping, count how many times it chirps in 14 seconds. Add 40 to that number. The total should be close to the actual temperature, in Fahrenheit. (For Celsius, count over 25 seconds, then divide by three, and add four.)

WHAT IS CLIMATE?

You may live in an area that gets a ton of snow in the winter. But your cousin might live in a place where it's hot and they wear shorts for most of the year. What's up? Why the difference?

Different areas, or **regions**, have different weather patterns. What we call "weather" is really something that we measure over a short period of time—was it raining yesterday? Is it hot today? Climate is measured over many, many years.

WORDS TO KNOW

region: a large area of the earth.

species: a group of plants or animals that are related and look the same.

adapt: to change in order to survive.

environment: the area in which something lives.

HOME SWEET HOME

Plants and animals live in every type of climate, from lush rainforests to hot, dry deserts to icy-cold polar regions. But you won't find a camel in the rainforest, or a cactus in the Arctic. That's because plant and animal **species** have **adapted** to live in specific **environments** and can't survive extreme changes.

When you think of Africa, what kind of weather do you think of? Probably hot and dry. What about the North Pole? Brr! Cold and snowy. That's the climate of those areas. But on any one day, it could rain in the desert of Africa, or even be chilly. That's called weather. But the general trend, or climate, is hot and dry.

WORDS TO KNOW

climate zone: a large region with a similar climate.

There are different **climate zones** around the world. Generally, they're separated by the air temperatures and the amount of precipitation an area gets. The earth is divided into three basic climate zones: tropical, temperate, and polar.

TROPICAL: This zone lies along the earth's equator. The tropical zone is hotter than areas further north and south of the equator because it gets the most direct sunlight. The climate in tropical zones can either be dry or humid—for example, a desert or a rainforest.

TEMPERATE: Temperate zones have temperatures that may vary, but they don't get too hot or too cold for long. Most of the United States and Europe has a temperate climate.

POLAR: Polar zones can be found near the top and bottom of the earth. Places like Antarctica, Alaska, and Greenland are all in a polar zone. These areas get the least direct sunlight, so their climates are the coldest.

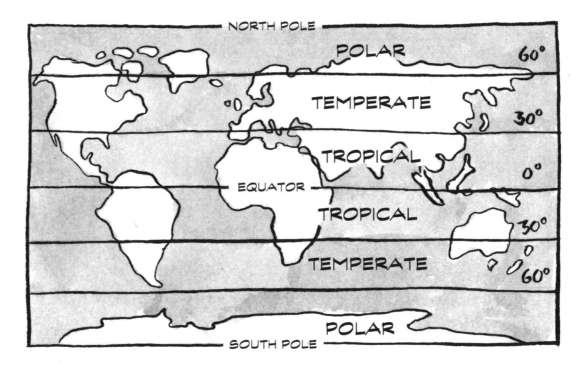

EDIBLE CLIMATE ZONE MAP

The world has many different types of climates. The United States has several different climates as well. With this edible map, you can tell your family about summer climates—after you chew.

SUPPLIES

- pizza or sugar cookie dough
- pizza toppings such as sauce, ham cubes, olives, pepperoni, pineapple, different cheeses, mushrooms, or bell peppers
- sugar cookie toppings such as chocolate chips, shredded coconut, nuts, or colored candy

1 Take a good look at the climate zone map shown here of the United States. Mold your dough into the shape of the United States. (It doesn't have to be perfect!)

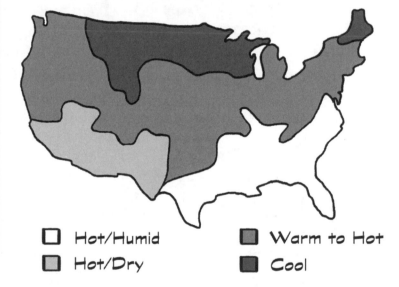

☐ Hot/Humid   ☐ Warm to Hot

☐ Hot/Dry   ☐ Cool

2 If you're making pizza, cover the entire country with sauce and a layer of cheese. Now you're ready to create your climates.

3 There are four general climate areas in the United States: hot/humid, hot/dry, warm to hot, and cool. Use one topping for each climate zone.

4 Bake according to your pizza or sugar cookie recipe, and share with your family.

WEATHER GAME

SUPPLIES

- index cards
- markers, crayons, or colored pencils
- large piece of paper or poster board (or several pieces of paper taped together)
- small figures or drawings to use as playing pieces

This is a quick game you can play with your family that shows how the weather affects many of your outdoor activities. As you play, talk about how you might adapt some of your upcoming plans if you get unexpected weather!

1 On several index cards, draw pictures representing a different weather event—sunshine, rain, thunderstorm, snow, wind, extreme weather (like a tornado), cold temperatures, steamy hot, and so on. The more you can think of, the better. Write "Weather Card" on the blank side of each index card. Set these cards to one side.

2 Take some more index cards and draw pictures (or write descriptions) of outdoor activities on them. Try to think of as many activities as possible—skiing, swimming, splashing in puddles, flying a kite, catching snowflakes on your tongue, having a picnic, riding your bike, and so on. Write "Activity Card" on the blank side of each of these index cards.

3 Put the cards aside and get out the paper. This will be your game board. Make a starting point and an end. Draw a winding path around the board from the start to the end. Then divide the path into individual squares. You'll move your playing pieces along these squares. You probably don't want too many squares, or the game will take too long.

4 Take the Weather Cards and place them face down in the middle of the board. Then take the Activity Cards and place them face down in a separate pile.

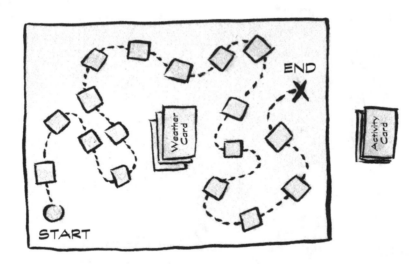

5 Begin with everyone's playing piece at the start. To play, pick an Activity Card and a Weather Card. If the activity is something you could do in those weather conditions, move your piece forward a square. If you can't do the activity in the weather conditions, you don't get to move. Just put the cards down and the next person picks.

6 If you run out of cards, shuffle each deck and keep going through them. The first person to reach the finish wins.

RAIN STICK

**Do you love to listen to the sound of the rain?
By making your own rain stick, you can hear the
rain any time you like—without even getting wet!**

HAVE AN ADULT HELP WITH THE NAILS.

SUPPLIES

- ○ long cardboard tube
  (wrapping-paper tubes
  are the best, but you
  can use a paper towel
  tube, or even duct tape
  several paper towel
  tubes together)
- ○ marker
- ○ 1-inch nails (2½
  centimeters), with the
  amount depending on
  the length of your tube
- ○ duct tape
- ○ colored paper
- ○ dry rice and/or dry
  beans
- ○ stickers

1 There's a spiral seam that runs the length of your cardboard tube. Using the marker, make dots all the way down the tube just about a half inch above this seam (1 centimeter). The marks will be where you put the nails. If you put the nails right on the seam, the tube can split. Make your marks about a half inch apart from each other (1 centimeter).

2 With an adult helping, poke a nail into each dot carefully. The nail should not go all the way through to the other side of the tube.

3 Run a piece of duct tape around and around the tube, covering the nail heads and holding them in place.

4 Cut a piece of paper large enough to cover the openings on the ends of the tube. Cover one end and tape the paper in place.

5 Pour the dry rice or beans in the open end. You can also use a little of both. You'll want about a handful in the tube, depending on the length. For now, cover the open end with your hand and turn the rain stick over to hear the sound. If you want more noise, add more beans or rice.

6 When you have the sound you want, use the other piece of paper to cover the open end of the tube and tape it closed.

7 Decorate the tube with markers, stickers, or colored paper. To hear the rain, just turn your rain stick over from end to end!

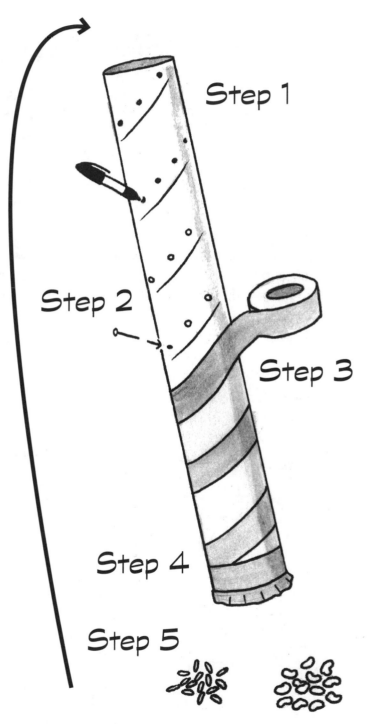

Step 1

Step 2

Step 3

Step 4

Step 5

WEATHER PREDICTION CHART

SUPPLIES
○ markers
○ poster board

Weather forecasters use complex weather instruments and computers to help them predict the weather. You can use an easier method by making a weather prediction chart. See how accurate your predictions really are!

1 Using the markers, make three columns on the poster board. Label the first column "Day," the second "My Prediction," and the third "Actual Weather."

2 Divide each column into seven rows. You'll keep track for an entire week, so label each row with a day of the week.

DAY	MY PREDICTION	ACTUAL WEATHER
M		
T		
W		
T		
F		
S		
S		

3 On the first day, look outside and make observations. Look at the sayings on pages 7, 8, and 9. They can help you figure out what to look for. What do your observations mean? For example, if you see the leaves curling on an oak tree, you can write, "rain coming" in the "My Prediction" column.

4 On the next day, write what really happened in the "Actual Weather" column. Did the rain really come? Did you miss a sign, or were you right on target?

5 Continue for the rest of the week, and see how your weather predictions measure up. Don't be discouraged if you miss some—even professional weather forecasters are wrong sometimes!

DOPPLER EFFECT EXPERIMENT

Doppler radar works because it measures changes in the sound of the signal that returns after it hits an object. You can see how this works with this simple experiment.

SUPPLIES

- battery-powered razor, or other object that makes a constant sound or buzz
- recording device, such as a computer, smart phone, or digital sound recorder
- tuning fork (optional)
- string (optional)

1 Turn on the razor or other object and record it. Then, play back your recording. It should sound like the normal thing.

2 Turn on the object again and record it a second time. This time though, move it close to the recorder and then move it farther away while you are recording.

3 Play back the sound. You should hear the sound change its pitch—it sounds like it gets higher pitched as it gets closer and lower pitched as it moves away again. That's one of the ways Doppler radar works. It measures the difference in sound so you know if something is moving closer or farther away.

4 You can also tie a string to a tuning fork, if you have one. Sometimes the music or science room at school has tuning forks. Have someone tap the tuning fork. First listen to it normally. Then, have someone tap it again and swing it around their head. You'll hear the sound change pitch as it's going around and around.

TEMPERATURE

What's your favorite time of year? Maybe you like the summer, when you can spend long days outside, go swimming, and eat ice-cold popsicles. Or maybe it's the autumn, when you can pick apples and crunch through fallen leaves. Do you like to zoom down hills on skis in winter, or plant a garden in the spring? As the temperature changes along with the seasons, so do your favorite outdoor activities.

DID YOU KNOW?
The lowest temperature ever recorded on Earth was -129 degrees Fahrenheit, in Antarctica. That's -89.5 degrees Celsius. Brrrr!

LET'S TALK TEMPERATURE

How do you know what the temperature is outside? You look at the **thermometer**, of course. Many thermometers today are **digital**, but traditionally they're made from glass tubes that contain **mercury**. When it's hot, the mercury warms up and **expands**, rising up the tube. When it's cold, the mercury **contracts**, and falls down the tube.

TEMPERATURE CAN BE MEASURED ON THREE DIFFERENT SCALES:

* **FAHRENHEIT:** If you're in the United States, people use Fahrenheit to measure temperature. On this **scale**, water freezes at 32 degrees and boils at 212 degrees.

* **CELSIUS:** Most other countries in the world use Celsius to measure temperature. On the Celsius scale, water freezes at 0 degrees and boils at 100.

* **KELVIN:** Scientists use a scale called Kelvin. On this scale, zero is the coldest temperature anything can possibly be. Water freezes at 273 K and boils at 373 K. (The "K" stands for Kelvin).

WORDS TO KNOW

thermometer: a weather instrument used to measure temperature.

digital: when a device shows information as numbers.

mercury: a liquid metal used inside thermometers.

expand: to spread out and take up more space.

contract: to shrink and take up less space.

scale: a measuring system.

IS IT HOT IN HERE?

Sometimes it can feel hotter than the temperature you see on the thermometer. If there's a lot of moisture in the air, it's humid. Humidity can make you feel even hotter than just the temperature of the air.

WORDS TO KNOW

heat index: the air temperature combined with the humidity in the air.

heat stroke: a condition when your body gets dangerously overheated.

When you're hot, you sweat. It's your body's way of getting rid of extra heat. Usually, the sweat on your skin evaporates into the air around you, cooling you down. But when it's really humid, there is already moisture in the air. So the moisture on your skin has trouble evaporating and it's hard for you to cool down.

DID YOU KNOW?

The highest temperature ever recorded was 136 degrees Fahrenheit (58 degrees Celsius). This was on September 13, 1922, in Libya, a country in northern Africa. That's a scorcher!

To let people know what the air outside will really feel like, scientists developed the **heat index**. The heat index combines the air temperature and the humidity. A very high heat index can be dangerous. It can lead to something called **heat stroke**. Your heart starts to pound fast and you feel dizzy. Heat stroke is serious, and you need to get help quickly if you feel the symptoms coming on when you're outside.

22

IF THE HEAT INDEX IS . . .	THE DANGER TO YOU IS . . .
90 to 105 degrees Fahrenheit (32 to 40 degrees Celsius)	heat stroke is **possible** if you're outside too long
105 to 130 degrees Fahrenheit (40 to 54 degrees Celsius)	heat stroke is **likely** if you're outside too long
130 degrees or higher Fahrenheit (above 54 degrees Celsius)	heat stroke is **highly likely** if you're outside too long

Fortunately, the weather forecasters are looking out for you. They'll issue these warnings to let you know when it's going to be a dangerously hot day:

* **HEAT ADVISORY:** A heat advisory means that the heat index is greater than 105 degrees Fahrenheit (40 degrees Celsius) and less than 115 degrees Fahrenheit (46 degrees Celsius).

* **EXCESSIVE HEAT WATCH:** An excessive heat watch means that the heat index *may* be 115 degrees Fahrenheit (46 degrees Celsius) or greater for a few days.

* **EXCESSIVE HEAT WARNING:** An excessive heat warning means that the heat index *will* be greater than 115 degrees Fahrenheit (46 degrees Celsius) for at least two days in a row.

DID YOU KNOW?
Climate is affected by the ocean and by altitude. Juneau, Alaska, has more warm days than Flagstaff, Arizona. That's because Juneau is warmed by its location near the sea, while Flagstaff is cooled by its higher elevation.

IT'S COLD OUT THERE!

Chances are you won't be seeing a heat index during the winter. But winter has its own measurement of how it really feels when you're outside—the **wind chill**.

WORDS TO KNOW

wind chill: what the combination of air temperature and wind feels like on your skin.

You've probably noticed that you feel cooler when it's windy. The wind chill combines the temperature of the air with the amount of wind. Suppose it's 5 degrees Fahrenheit outside (-15 degrees Celsius). That's pretty cold! But if the wind is blowing at 5 miles per hour, then it really feels like it's -5 degrees Fahrenheit (-20 Celsius). And if the wind is blowing at 20 miles per hour, then it really feels like -15 degrees Fahrenheit (-26 degrees Celsius)! See what a difference the wind can make?

Once again, the weather forecasters have your back. They'll issue alerts to let you know if it's dangerously cold outside:

* **WIND CHILL ADVISORY:** A wind chill advisory means that the wind chill is expected to be between -15 degrees and -24 degrees Fahrenheit (-26 to -31 degrees Celsius).

* **WIND CHILL WARNING:** A wind chill warning means that the wind chill is expected to be lower than -25 degrees Fahrenheit (below -32 degrees Celsius).

TEMPERATURE

PUFF, PUFF, PUFF

Ever wonder why you can see your breath when it's cold outside? That's because your breath is warm and humid (it has evaporated water in it). When your warm breath hits the cold air, the moisture in it instantly gets colder and denser. This result is the little cloud you see.

HEAT ME UP!

The sun makes life possible in so many ways. It gives us light, helps plants grow, and even keeps us healthy. But perhaps the most important thing the sun does is give us warmth.

All weather begins with the sun. The sun doesn't just keep us warm— it warms the air around us, too. And warm air makes weather events happen. As air gets heated by the sun, it either rises or falls. This movement of the air creates wind. You'll read more about the movement of air in Chapter 3. For now, just remember the sun's warmth really gets our atmosphere moving!

DID YOU KNOW?

If you like the cold, go to Barrow, Alaska, because it has an average of 321 days a year when it's colder than 32 degrees Fahrenheit (below 0 degrees Celsius). And that's without the wind chill factored in!

CHANGING SEASONS

Why do we have spring, summer, autumn, and winter? Because the earth is tilted slightly as it follows its **orbit** around the sun. This means that when one hemisphere of the earth is facing the sun, the other hemisphere is tipped away from it.

WORDS TO KNOW

orbit: the path a planet takes around the sun.

mild: not too hot and not too cold.

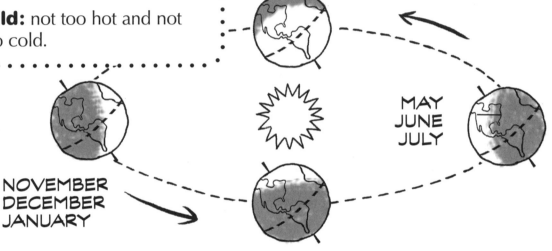

MAY JUNE JULY

NOVEMBER DECEMBER JANUARY

In May, June, and July, it's summer in the Northern Hemisphere and winter in the Southern Hemisphere. This is because the Northern Hemisphere is facing the warm sun more directly. During summer, the days are long and warm. In November, December, and January, the Southern Hemisphere is more directly facing the sun and has summer. Meanwhile, it is winter in the Northern Hemisphere. In spring and autumn, temperatures are **mild** most places. Except for the equator, the rest of the earth is not facing the sun directly. It isn't hidden from the sun's rays for much of the day either, so it's not as cold as winter or as hot as summer.

EXTREME CLIMATES

Some climates are extremely hot or cold. Desert regions, for example, experience very high temperatures. At night, though, the temperatures in some deserts can drop below freezing! That's because there are no trees, grass, or other plants to capture and hold the sun's heat from the day.

Places near the equator are extremely hot. That's because they get more direct sunlight than anywhere else on Earth. The equator never tilts away from the sun. For example, northern Africa gets a relentless beating of the sun. This is because of its position along the equator and a steady pattern of high air pressure. It's almost constantly sunny and hot, with extremely little rainfall.

On the other hand, Polar Regions get very little direct sunlight (if any). So the temperature plummets and can stay freezing for months.

DID YOU KNOW?

In India, people recognize six seasons instead of four: spring, summer, **monsoon**, autumn, pre-winter, and winter. Each season is about two months long.

WORDS TO KNOW

monsoon: a wind that brings heavy rainfall to southern Asia in summer.

SUN CATCHERS

Whether it's hot or cold outside, you can celebrate the sunshine coming in through the windows with these easy-to-make sun catchers.

SUPPLIES

- wax paper
- white glue
- paper plate
- scissors
- yarn
- food coloring
- toothpick

1 Lay a large piece of wax paper out as your work surface.

2 Pour a little bit of glue onto a paper plate.

3 Cut a piece of yarn about a foot long (30 centimeters), and run it through the glue. Gently "pinch" off any excess glue by running the yarn between your finger and thumb. You want the yarn to have enough glue on it to make it stiff, but not dripping and sloppy.

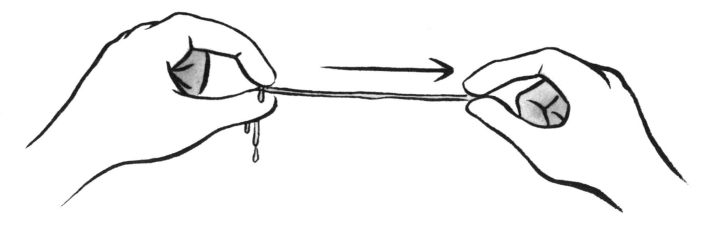

4 Arrange your yarn on the wax paper in whatever shape you want—like a star or a heart, for example. Make sure the ends of the yarn are touching each other. You want a completely closed shape. Let it dry completely.

5 Cut a smaller piece of yarn. Once the shape is dry, carefully lift one edge of the shape and tie a short loop of yarn around it. This loop will be used for hanging your sun catcher. Then press your shape back down onto the wax paper. If it's lifting up even a little, glue will leak out during the next step.

6 Pour more glue out on the paper plate and add a few drops of food coloring. Use the toothpick to blend the glue and food coloring. Then pour the glue onto the wax paper into the space of your shape. Use the toothpick to push it around until the inside of your shape is completely filled.

7 Let your sun catcher dry completely, then gently pull the wax paper off the back of it. Now you're ready to hang your sun catcher in a sunny window!

8 Try making more shapes. You can divide them with yarn into more than one section. Then make each section a different color.

ANGLE OF THE SUN EXPERIMENT

SUPPLIES

- ○ white paper
- ○ freezer
- ○ wall, or other place to prop the clipboard
- ○ strong flashlight that produces some heat when it's shining
- ○ short stack of books, about 2 inches tall (5 centimeters)
- ○ clipboard
- ○ pencil

This experiment shows why places like the equator, where the sun shines down directly, are very hot. Places where the sun shines at an angle, like all of the United States, have less extreme heat.

1 Put the paper in the freezer for about 15 minutes. Meanwhile, place the stack of books 2 inches away from the wall (about 5 centimeters). Lie the flashlight on the books and turn it on so it is shining directly at the wall.

2 Take the paper out of the freezer and quickly clip it to the clipboard. Prop up the clipboard against the wall so the flashlight is shining on it. Make it as straight as possible.

3 Draw a circle around the beam of light on the paper, trying not to touch any other part of the paper.

4 After about 10 seconds, turn the flashlight off, and feel the paper where the light hit. Then feel the paper just outside the circle, and then farther away. The paper gets cooler the farther away from where the flashlight hit.

5 Put the paper back in the freezer. After 15 minutes, bring it back out and put it on the clipboard again.

6 This time, prop the clipboard against the wall at an angle, so it tips away from the flashlight. Then shine the flashlight on the paper, and draw a circle around the beam of light again.

7 After 10 seconds, turn the light off and feel the paper again. It should feel less warm than the first time.

8 Look at the circles you drew around the light. The first time, the circle was smaller, but the heat was more intense. The second time, the circle was wider and not as hot.

DID YOU KNOW?
Light from the sun travels almost 93 million miles (145 million kilometers) and reaches Earth in only eight minutes! This is called the speed of light.

SEASONS EXPERIMENT

SUPPLIES

- ○ lamp with a removable shade
- ○ globe or large ball

This experiment will help you understand why we would not have seasons if the earth wasn't tilted. Look at the picture on page 26 to see how to hold your earth and move it around your sun.

1 Place the lamp on a table or the floor, making sure it's on a stable surface. Remove the shade and turn the light on. This is your "sun."

2 Stand a couple of feet away (a meter or less), holding the globe. This is your "Earth." Tip the globe slightly in your hands, so the top is tilting toward the lamp.

3 Look at how the light hits the globe. The part that's tipped toward the light (the top half of the globe) is experiencing summer. The bottom half is in winter.

4 Keeping the tilt at the same angle, walk one-quarter of the way around the light. Now it's spring in the Southern Hemisphere and autumn in the Northern Hemisphere.

5 Walk another quarter of the way around the light, so you're standing opposite where you started. The southern part of your globe is now in summer, and the northern part is in winter.

6 Finish the experiment by walking another quarter of the way around the light. It's now spring in the Northern Hemisphere and autumn in the Southern Hemisphere.

THERMOMETER

SUPPLIES

- clear plastic bottle
- water
- rubbing alcohol
- food coloring
- modeling clay
- clear drinking straw

Thermometers work when the air temperature warms or cools the liquid inside the tube. When the liquid is heated it expands and rises up the tube. When the liquid is cooled it contracts and falls down the tube. With this project, you can watch a thermometer at work.

1 Fill the bottle about one-quarter of the way full with a mix of half water and half rubbing alcohol. Add a few drops of food coloring. This will make the liquid easier to see.

2 Wrap a wad of clay around one end of the straw. Put the other end of the straw into the bottle, but don't let it touch the bottom. Slide the clay farther down the straw if you need to keep it from touching the bottom.

3 Warm the liquid by holding the bottle very still between both of your hands. As the liquid gets warm, it expands. Watch as the liquid rises up through the straw.

If you've ever watched a weather forecast on television, you've probably seen a big map with lots of lines and symbols. And you might have heard the weather forecaster saying things like, "An area of high pressure will be building up and moving over our area." It sounds so confusing and you just want to know whether to bring your umbrella to school or not. But air pressure actually can tell us what kind of weather to expect.

When forecasters talk about air pressure, they're referring to how strongly the atmosphere is pressing down toward the surface of the earth. It's hard to believe something invisible like air has any weight to press down on anything. After all, air is around you all the time, but you don't feel it.

AIR PRESSURE

You can do a quick experiment with balloons to see that air has weight. If you hang two full balloons from each end of a stick, and then hang the stick like a balance, the balloons will weigh the same. But if you let air out of one balloon, the balance will tip toward the balloon full of air—because air has weight.

Just like with mercury in a thermometer, when air warms up, it rises, and when it cools down, it falls. This is because when air warms, its molecules start moving faster and spread farther apart. This makes the air less dense and it rises. The opposite happens when air is cooled. Warm masses of air move up while cool masses of air press down.

Some places on Earth are always warmer than others. Things like day or night, the tilt of the earth, and how different surfaces absorb sunlight—such as rocks, trees, or water—all affect air temperature. Air is always moving around between areas of cold air and areas of warm air to try to even out its temperature. This causes changes in air pressure. And air pressure affects the weather.

DID YOU KNOW?

Your whole body is under about 15 pounds of pressure per square inch (1 kilogram per square centimeter). You don't feel it because you have air pressure inside your body that balances the pressure from outside.

"HIGH" THERE, PRESSURE!

If you hear the weather forecaster say an area of high pressure is coming your way, you can keep your umbrella in the closet. High-pressure systems form when there is a pocket of air that is cooler than the rest of the air around it. When air cools, its molecules huddle closer together. This makes the air more dense and it shrinks.

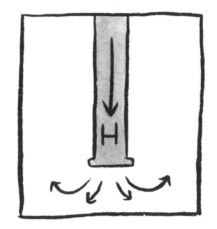

When a pocket of air shrinks, it leaves space around it that gets filled in by more air. As air moves in to fill the space, it presses down toward the surface of the earth where you are. The force of the air rushing in breaks up clouds and you get clear, sunny days. This is why high-pressure systems are also called "fair weather systems."

BAROMETRIC PRESSURE

Scientists use a weather instrument called a barometer to measure the amount of pressure in the air. There are different kinds of barometers, but they work pretty much the same way. A long, glass tube is placed with one end in a cup of liquid metal, like mercury. When air presses down on the liquid in the cup, some of it gets forced up into the tube. The higher the air pressure, the higher the liquid rises in the tube. You can look at a barometer to see if air pressure is high or low. You can also use a barometer to track whether air pressure is rising or falling.

AIR PRESSURE

THE LOW DOWN ON LOW PRESSURE

A low-pressure system is a whirling mass of warm, moist air. Warm air rises and the air that moves in to fill the space left behind is moving up away from the earth's surface and not pressing down. So the air pressure is called "low" and it's time to grab that umbrella!

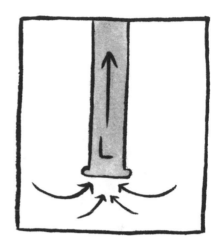

The higher the mass of warm air rises, the more it thins. As air gets thinner, it can't hold as much heat. It starts to cool by letting out moisture. This creates clouds, rainfall, precipitation, and other bad weather like tropical storms and cyclones.

WINDS OF CHANGE

All this air moving from one pressure system to another can only mean one thing—wind! Wind is air in motion. When one mass of air rises or falls, the space it leaves behind can't just be left empty. Another mass of air rushes in to fill it. This movement of air is what we feel as wind.

When the sun is shining, the air above the land gets heated up faster than the air above the sea. When warm air from over the land rises, cooler air from above the sea fills in the space left behind. This is what makes those sea breezes that feel so good on a hot summer afternoon at the beach!

THERE'S A FRONT COMING!

When warm air and cold air meet, they create a front. When you see a weather map on TV, it's usually covered with lines and symbols showing where different kinds of fronts are happening. Anywhere you see a front, there will be precipitation. If warm air meets up with cold air, it rises over the cold air and starts to cool down. If cold air meets up with warm air, it pushes up the warm air. You know what happens when warm air rises—stormy weather!

FRONT SYMBOL	WHAT IT MEANS . . .
COLD	A **cold front** means a cold air mass is moving in the direction of the triangles. The temperature drops and there's a chance of rain.
WARM	A **warm front** means a warm air mass is moving in the direction of the semi-circles. It will get warmer and also may bring rain.
STATIONARY	Cold and warm air masses aren't always strong enough to move each other. A front can stay in the same place for days. This is called a **stationary front**. Cold air is on the semi-circle side trying to push to the other side, and warm air is stuck on the triangle side. Clouds and precipitation are likely.
OCCLUDED	When a fast-moving front catches up to a slower-moving front, it's called an **occluded front**. You'll feel wind and a quick change in temperature.

HIGH ON A MOUNTAINTOP

Temperature change isn't the only thing that affects air pressure. So does altitude. There's far less air pressure on top of a mountain than down by the sea. That's because the lower you are, the more air there is above you. Remember, air has weight and presses down on you. But if you go higher up, there's less air above you pressing down.

Do you know what less air pressure would mean for you if you tried to climb Mount Everest? When air pressure is low, the molecules in the air are more spread out. And what kinds of molecules are in the air? The oxygen molecules you need to breathe! So with each breath you take, you grab less oxygen because the oxygen molecules are all spread out. If you climb slowly, your body can adjust to the lower air pressure. Your heart will beat faster, your breathing will be faster, and your body will make more of the red blood cells it needs to carry oxygen around your body. If you climb too high, too fast, you can feel sick and get headaches. This is known as altitude sickness.

AIR PRESSURE EXPERIMENT

This fun experiment illustrates the power of air pressure. Do this for friends and family to help them understand air pressure, too!

HAVE AN ADULT HELP YOU WITH THE MATCH.

SUPPLIES

- ○ hard-boiled egg
- ○ glass bottle with a wide neck, such as an old-fashioned milk bottle
- ○ match

1 Peel the shell off the hard-boiled egg.

2 Have an adult light a match and then toss it inside the bottle. As soon as the match is in, quickly set the small end of the egg down on the mouth of the bottle.

3 Watch what happens. Because the flame from the match uses up some of the air inside the bottle, the air pressure in the bottle gets lower. Meanwhile, the air outside the bottle has a higher pressure. The area of higher pressure tries to move into the area of lower pressure inside the bottle. It presses down on the egg, and the egg gets popped into the bottle.

AIR WARMING EXPERIMENT

SUPPLIES

○ empty plastic bottle
○ balloon
○ water
○ pot big enough to fit the bottle lying down
○ stove

This experiment illustrates how air rises and expands when it's warmed up.

HAVE AN ADULT HELP WITH THE HOT WATER

1 Stretch the balloon over the mouth of the bottle. Set aside.

2 Fill the pot half full with water. Have an adult heat the water until it's very hot but not boiling.

3 Carefully put the bottle into the hot water (have an adult hold it in if necessary). After a while, the balloon will begin to inflate. Why? Because the air inside the bottle is heating up. As it heats up, the air molecules start moving faster and spread farther apart. As they expand, the air molecules move out of the bottle and into the balloon, inflating it. It's still the same amount of air that you started with, but now it's taking up more space.

WINDSOCK

Another instrument for measuring the wind is called a windsock. A windsock shows which direction the wind is coming from. In this project you'll make your own windsock to hang outside.

HAVE AN ADULT HELP YOU BEND THE COAT HANGER.

SUPPLIES

○ old, long-sleeved shirt
○ scissors
○ wire coat hanger
○ needle and thread
○ small rock or other weight
○ 4 pieces of string, each about a foot long (30 centimeters)
○ dowel, about 1½ feet long (about 45 centimeters)
○ compass

1 Cut a sleeve off the shirt.

2 Bend the coat hanger into a circle, the same size as the opening of the sleeve. Have an adult cut the wire if it's too long. Using the needle and thread, stitch the wire into the sleeve opening, so it's holding the sleeve open in a circle at one end.

3 Stitch the small rock or weight near the opening of the sleeve. This will give your windsock a little weight so it keeps facing the wind.

4 Sew each piece of string evenly spaced around the opening in the windsock. Tie the other end of each one to the top of the dowel.

5 Stick the other end of the dowel into the ground. When the wind blows, your windsock will puff up and show you which direction the wind is coming from. Use a compass to find out which direction is which, so next time you'll be able to tell just by looking at your windsock.

42

BAROMETER

One way you can predict the weather is by using a barometer. Barometers measure the air pressure around you. Keep track of the air pressure, and see what kind of weather happens the next day. After some practice, you might be able to make your own forecasts!

SUPPLIES

- ○ balloon
- ○ scissors
- ○ glass jar
- ○ rubber band
- ○ straw
- ○ tape
- ○ paper
- ○ marker

1 Stretch out the balloon by inflating and deflating it a few times. Cut off the neck of the balloon. Pull the balloon tight over the mouth of the jar, and hold it in place with the rubber band.

2 Tape one end of the straw on top of the balloon so that the other end sticks out one side.

3 Take the jar outside and put it up against a wall in a protected area, like a porch. Tape the paper to the wall behind it, and use the marker to make a mark where the straw points. This is your starting point.

4 Every day, see where the straw is pointing. When it moves up or down, mark those places on the paper, labeling them "high" (when it's above the original mark) or "low" (when it's below it). When the air outside the jar presses down on the balloon (high air pressure), it will make the straw go up. The opposite happens when the air pressure outside the jar is low.

5 You can now try to predict what the weather will be like by looking at your barometer!

ANEMOMETER

Windy weather usually means that one air mass is leaving, and a different one is taking its place. You can see how fast the wind is blowing with a weather instrument called an anemometer. In this project you'll make your own anemometer to put outside. You'll be able to see how windy it is just by looking out your window.

SUPPLIES

- paper punch
- 5 small paper cups
- scissors
- 2 straws
- stapler
- pin or tack
- pencil with eraser
- pot or bowl filled with potting soil (optional)

1 Using the paper punch, poke one hole in four of the paper cups, about $\frac{1}{2}$ inch below the rim (about $1\frac{1}{2}$ centimeters). On the fifth cup, punch four equally spaced holes about $\frac{1}{4}$ inch below the rim (a little less than 1 centimeter). Then, poke a hole in the center of the bottom of each cup with the scissors.

2 Push a straw through the hole from the outside into one of the four cups until it touches the other side of the cup. Fold some of the straw over inside the cup and staple it in place on the far side of the cup. Take the second straw and do the same thing in a second cup.

3 Slide the free end of one of the straws through two opposite holes in the fifth cup. Then, connect one of the remaining cups onto the same straw. Slide it onto the straw until the straw hits the far side. Make sure the outside cups face opposite directions. Staple the straw inside the cup.

4 Repeat with the last two cups. Slide the free end of the straw stapled into a cup through opposite holes in the fifth cup. Then slide it through the last empty cup. With the outside cups facing opposite directions, staple the straw to the last cup.

5 Arrange the four cups so they're all going the same direction around the center cup. Then, push the pin through the two straws where they cross over each other.

6 Push the pencil, eraser end first, through the bottom hole in the center cup. Push the pin into the eraser as far as it will go.

7 Your anemometer is ready! Push the pencil into the ground in an area where the cups can spin freely without hitting anything. When the wind blows, it will spin your cups. The stronger the wind, the faster your anemometer will spin. If you want your anemometer higher up off the ground, push the pencil into a pot or bowl full of potting soil. Than you can move your anemometer easily to catch the best wind.

PRECIPITATION

WORDS TO KNOW

recycle: to use something again.

glacier: a huge mass of ice and snow.

water cycle: the natural recycling of water.

evaporate: when a liquid turns into a gas.

Can you believe the rain that falls today is the same rain that fell on the tyrannosaurus rex back in the days of the dinosaurs? That's because all the water on Earth is always **recycling**. This includes the water in oceans and rivers, and even water locked in **glaciers**.

The water we have now is all the water we'll ever have. Water never goes away—but it changes form. Water changes from a liquid to a gas and back again, over and over and over again. These changes are all part of the **water cycle**. When water is heated by the sun it **evaporates**. This means it turns from a liquid into a gas and disappears into the air.

PRECIPITATION

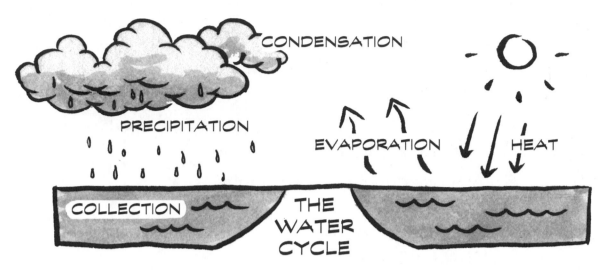

CONDENSATION

PRECIPITATION

EVAPORATION · HEAT

COLLECTION

THE WATER CYCLE

When water enters the air it's called **water vapor**. Water vapor is invisible, but it's all around you! The amount of water vapor in the air changes all the time. If there isn't a lot of water vapor, the air feels dry. A lot of water vapor in the air feels sticky. This is humidity. Sometimes there's so much water vapor in the air that you get wet—because it's raining!

WORDS TO KNOW

water vapor: the gas form of water when it's evaporated in the air.

condense: when water vapor turns into liquid water.

gravity: a force that pulls objects to the earth.

Rain happens when water vapor rises high into the atmosphere. Remember, it's cold up there, so the water vapor starts to change back into water. It **condenses** and sticks together, forming water drops or ice crystals. This makes the water visible again—as clouds! The drops in the clouds get bigger until they're too heavy to stay in the air. Then **gravity** pulls them toward the earth as precipitation, like rain or snow. The liquid collects in oceans, rivers, or lakes, or ends up on land and soaks into the ground.

THE RAINBOW CONNECTION

Have you ever seen a rainbow? How about a double rainbow? And is there really a pot of gold at the end?

You usually only see a rainbow after it rains. That's because rainbows are created when sunlight hits raindrops that are still suspended in the air. To see a rainbow, the sun has to be behind you, and the raindrops in front of you.

Light is made up of different colors, although you don't usually see all these colors at the same time. But in a rainbow, light is split up into its different colors, and you can see them all at once! The colors of a rainbow are always in the same pattern: red, orange, yellow, green, blue, indigo, and violet.

When there is a double rainbow, the second one is above and outside the first one. Its colors are in the same order but reversed. Red is on the inside at the bottom and violet is on the outside at the top.

RED
ORANGE
YELLOW
GREEN
BLUE
INDIGO
VIOLET

Now, about the gold. Unfortunately, rainbows aren't physical things—you can't touch them. So it's impossible to put a pot of gold at the end of a rainbow. But that doesn't mean you can't feel lucky when you see one!

PRECIPITATION

SNOW

Do you love the fist snowfall each year? Some snow is wet and sticky, perfect for packing snowballs or making snowmen. Then there's light, fluffy snow, easy to shovel from the sidewalk. Sometimes a hard, crusty surface covers softer snow underneath. If the crust is thick enough, you can walk right on top of the snow. The type of snow that falls depends on the layers of warm and cold air that it passes through on the way to the ground.

DID YOU KNOW?
The largest snowflake ever recorded was in Montana back in 1887. It was a whopping 15 inches across (38 centimeters). Try catching that on your tongue!

A snowflake starts out high in the atmosphere as a tiny ice crystal. Then, droplets of moisture in the air begin sticking to the crystal, and freezing together. As more droplets stick to the crystal, it gets bigger and freezes into wonderful shapes.

Most snowflakes have six main arms, and the patterns that form within the crystal are often very fancy—and beautiful. It's unlikely that any two snowflakes will ever have the exact same pattern.

When the crystals get heavy enough they begin falling down toward the ground, and you've got snow!

SLEET? FREEZING RAIN? HAIL? HELP!

The most common types of precipitation are rain and snow. It's easy to tell them apart. But there's also sleet, freezing rain, and hail. It's not so easy to tell them apart, but here's how they are different:

SLEET

FREEZING RAIN

SLEET looks a bit like snow, but it bounces off the ground when it lands. These little white pellets begin as frozen precipitation very high in the atmosphere. Then they fall through a layer of warmer air where they melt. But before they hit the ground, they pass through a last layer of thick cold air, where the pellets freeze again. Because they turn to liquid and refreeze, they are not light and fluffy.

FREEZING RAIN begins just like sleet does. The difference is the thickness of the last layer of cold air. If it's too thin for the precipitation to freeze, it stays as rain that is very cold. It only freezes when it hits something.

Freezing rain doesn't bounce off the ground or cars—it lands and forms a layer of ice. Ice is heavy, and if enough of it forms on trees, they come crashing down—often taking down power lines with them. Freezing rain can cause a lot of damage!

PRECIPITATION

HAIL can look like small golf balls. It begins as tiny clumps of ice in thunderclouds. But these clumps of ice don't just fall to the ground. First they go through quite a bumpy ride inside the thundercloud! Wind takes them up and down, passing through layers of cool air and warm air. When the clumps of ice pass through the warm air, raindrops attach to them. Then when the wind catches them and lifts them up again through the cool air, they freeze.

HAIL

DID YOU KNOW?

The largest hailstone in recorded history was found in South Dakota in 2010. It was 8 inches across (20 centimeters), about as big as a soccer ball. And it was found after it had already melted a little!

This happens again and again, and the ice clumps get bigger and bigger—until they're hailstones. When the hailstones get too heavy, the wind can't carry them up again and they fall to the ground. Hailstones can get so large they actually damage property.

WORDS TO KNOW

- **drought:** a long period of time when there is too little rain.

- **sphere:** round, like a ball.

- **decade:** a 10-year period.

- **food chain:** plants and animals in an environment where each is eaten by another higher up in the chain.

DESERTS AND RAINFORESTS

If an area doesn't get rain for a long time, it's called a **drought**. Usually, high-pressure and low-pressure systems pass over an area and move on. Sometimes, though, a high-pressure system gets stuck and the air is only being pushed down and not up.

If air doesn't rise, it doesn't rain. This means nice, dry, sunny weather for days. But if it lasts a few weeks or years, it becomes a drought. Sometimes droughts even last a **decade** or more. Drought threatens plants, animals, and people, who all depend on the rain. After all, plants are the beginning of the **food chain**, so it's really important that they have enough water to grow or nothing can survive.

Some climates are used to little or no rain—like the desert. The animals and plants that live in these climates have adapted to the dry conditions that can often be extreme.

DID YOU KNOW?
Raindrops aren't really tear shaped, like you see in drawings. They're shaped more like **spheres**. Sometimes big raindrops can look a little flattened—like hamburger buns!

Look at the camel, for example. You may have heard they store water in the humps on their backs. That's not really true. A camel's hump actually stores fat deposits that the camel can use for energy. This makes camels able to go for long periods of time without the need for water. And camels can live with much higher temperatures than many other animals. They also have huge, wide feet to help them walk on the sand easily and long eyelashes to protect their eyes from blowing sand. They can even close their nostrils! But put that camel in the rainforest, and she'd be struggling to survive.

WORDS TO KNOW

canopy: up in the trees of the rainforest.

The sloth is an animal that's highly adapted to live high in the **canopy** of the rainforest. Its hair grows backward, from their stomach toward their back, to help the rain run off easily as the sloth hangs from its claws. And the sloth's stomach is divided into several sections to help it digest all the leaves it eats.

Plants are well developed to tolerate the weather conditions in their regions, too. Plants in the desert have to be able to collect and store the little water that falls there. Some plants in the rainforest have developed "air roots" to get the water they need from the humidity in the air, or from the rain directly, instead of from water that's absorbed into the ground.

MOUNTAIN CLIMB IT (ER, CLIMATE)

Because it gets colder the higher you go, the climate at the bottom of a big mountain is very different than the climate at the top.

Even though the distance from the bottom of a mountain to the top isn't always that great, the **ecosystem** can change dramatically as you go up. You could have a steamy jungle environment at the base of a mountain, and icy snow-capped peaks at the top. Plants and animals that live at the bottom often can't survive higher up.

WORDS TO KNOW

ecosystem: the plants and animals that make up an environment.

windward side: the side that faces into the oncoming winds.

The climate of either side of a mountain can be dramatically different as well. This is because the sheer size of mountains affects the weather. When air moves over oceans and lakes it picks up moisture evaporating from the water. The air then moves over the land. When the air hits a mountain, the wind lifts it so it can rise up and over the mountain. As air rises up one side of the mountain it thins and cools. When it cools, it drops moisture and that side of the mountain gets rain. This is called the **windward side**.

54

PRECIPITATION

By the time the clouds make it over the mountain, they've lost all their moisture and dried out. So the non-windy side of the mountain can be incredibly dry. This is called the **leeward side**. When an area that extends from the leeward side of a mountain doesn't get any rain, it's said to be in the **rain shadow** of the mountain. Sometimes these areas get so dry that they actually become desert. For example, the Gobi desert was formed because it's on the leeward side of the great Himalaya Mountain range in Asia.

WORDS TO KNOW

leeward side: the side that doesn't get hit by the traveling winds.

rain shadow: an area beside a mountain that gets little or no rain because it all fell on the mountain itself.

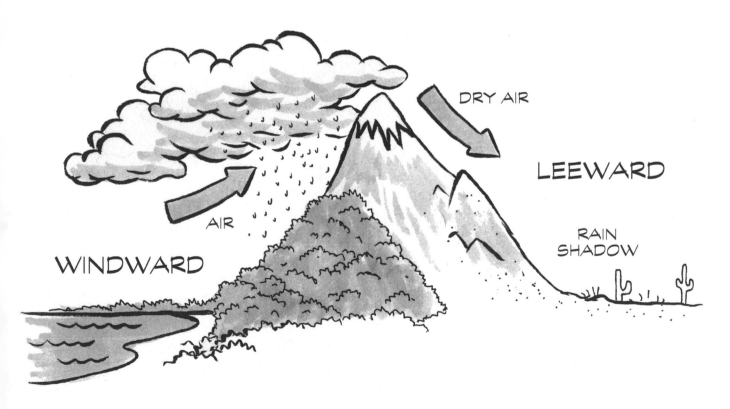

DRY AIR

LEEWARD

RAIN SHADOW

AIR

WINDWARD

WORLD MOUNTAINS AND THEIR RAIN SHADOWS

All over the world, you'll find rain shadows. Some are small, and others are quite large. They range from huge deserts, to a bustling city, to an island surrounded by water!

CONTINENT	MOUNTAINS	RAIN SHADOW
North America	Pacific Coast and Sierra Nevada Ranges	Death Valley
Hawaii	East Maui Volcano	Island of Kahoolawe
Europe	Mount Parnithia	Athens
Asia	The Himalayas	Tibetan Plateau
South America	The Andes	Atacama Desert
Africa	Atlas Mountains	Sahara Desert

RAIN GAUGE

SUPPLIES

- clear bottle or jar with straight sides
- ruler
- permanent marker

It's hard to tell how much rain is falling by looking outside. How do meteorologists know much rain has fallen? They use a rain gauge. In this project you'll make your own rain gauge so you can track the rainfall you receive at your house.

1 Remove any labels and make sure your bottle or jar is clean and dry.

2 Place the ruler against the jar. Using the marker, start at the bottom of your jar and measure up from the bottom, marking every $\frac{1}{4}$ inch ($\frac{1}{2}$ centimeter).

3 Set your rain gauge outside where there is nothing hanging over it to block the rain. If you think your gauge might tip over, you can bury it slightly in the ground, or brace it with stones or bricks on all four sides.

4 Check your gauge after each rain. You can even keep a log. Be sure to empty your gauge after every rainfall so you can get an accurate reading for the next one.

DID YOU KNOW?

There are some plants and animals that only live in specific rain shadows. The Devil's Hole pupfish, for example, is a tiny fish that only lives in the shallow pools of Death Valley.

SNOWFLAKE

Here's how to make a permanent snowflake to remind you of winter year-round! Hang it near a window to make it sparkle.

HAVE AN ADULT HELP YOU BOIL THE WATER.

SUPPLIES

- ○ pipe cleaners
- ○ scissors
- ○ wide-mouth glass jar
- ○ string
- ○ pencil
- ○ borax from the laundry detergent section of the store—look for "20 Mule Team Borax Laundry Booster" (you can use salt or sugar, but it takes longer)
- ○ boiling water
- ○ blue food coloring (optional)

1 Cut a pipe cleaner into 4 equal pieces. Twist them together in the middle and spread out the ends to form your snowflake shape. Make sure your snowflake will fit inside the jar.

2 Cut a piece of string. Tie one end to your snowflake and the other to your pencil. The string needs to be long enough for the snowflake to hang from the pencil inside the jar, but don't let it touch the bottom of the jar. Adjust the string until it's the right length. Then put the snowflake aside for now.

3 In the jar, mix the borax with the boiling water. Use three tablespoons of borax for every cup of water (240 milliliters). Stir well. You might have some borax sitting at the bottom of your jar. That's okay—just make sure you've stirred really well. Add the food coloring to the water if you want.

4 Hang your snowflake in the jar, and leave it there overnight. In the morning, crystals will have formed on it, making a beautiful snowflake!

RAIN

You don't have to do a rain dance to make it rain. With this experiment, you can see how rain forms in the atmosphere.

HAVE AN ADULT HELP YOU THE HEAT WATER.

SUPPLIES

- glass jar
- hot water—NOT boiling
- plate
- ice cubes

1 Remove any labels from your jar so that you have a clear view.

2 Have an adult warm up enough water to pour several inches into the glass jar (about 8 centimeters). Be sure it's not boiling water, or the jar will break.

3 Place the plate on top of the jar to seal it. Put the ice cubes on top of the plate, and watch for several minutes to see what happens.

4 Drops of water will start forming on the bottom of the plate. It's similar to what happens up in the atmosphere. Water vapor (like the steam rising from your hot water) rises and meets colder temperatures higher up (like the ice-cold plate). Then the water vapor condenses and turns back into liquid form—rain!

RAINBOW

SUPPLIES

- drinking glass
- water
- sunny day or flashlight
- white paper

Everyone is excited when a rainbow emerges in the sky. If you want to see a rainbow, you don't have to wait for one to appear outside. This project will show you how to make your own rainbow—inside!

1 Fill the glass with water until it's about three quarters full.

2 Stand next to a window where the sun is shining through, or use your flashlight.

3 Hold the white paper on the other side of the glass, and let the light shine through the water. The water will break up the light into all its colors, and a rainbow will form on your paper!

LIGHT

4 You can experiment with different angles for the water and the light to see what effect that has on your rainbow.

CLOUDS

Like rainbows, clouds can be fun to look at too. They are always moving and changing. Try lying on your back in the grass and watching clouds. They can form into any shape that your imagination can dream up!

Not all clouds are great for daydreaming, though. Some clouds carry dangerous lightning. Others might carry hail. But they all carry a message, and you can learn how to read those messages by learning "cloud language." For example, a wispy, light cloud high up in the sky is telling you that the weather is going to be great today. But a tall, thick cloud is warning you that a storm is coming.

WHAT IS A CLOUD?

Clouds are made up of water—water vapor and ice crystals to be exact. We've seen that when water vapor rises into the air, it starts getting cooler and condensing back into a liquid, or water droplets. These droplets begin to cling to tiny dust specks that are floating around in the sky. Soon more and more droplets form. When several billion of these droplets exist, you can see them in the sky—as a cloud.

Clouds are white because they're reflecting all the colors in the light from the sun. When clouds get dense with water droplets, all the light can't get through and they turn grey, or almost black. That usually means they're getting ready to drop their water down on you!

Do you know that there are many kinds of clouds—and each has its own name? Cirrus, stratus, and cumulus are common types of clouds. Each cloud looks different and tells us something about the weather.

DID YOU KNOW?
Other planets have clouds, too. Venus has lots of clouds. But those clouds are made up of poisonous gases. No cloud-gazing there!

CLOUD "LANGUAGE"

These are three types of clouds you probably see a lot. There are many other types too. A nimbus cloud, which has rain or snow already falling, means thunder and lightning could be coming soon!

IF IT LOOKS LIKE . . .	IT MEANS . . .
Thin, wispy clouds like streamers that are high in the sky.	**Cirrus:** The weather is nice, but a change in the weather is coming within 24 hours.
Gray clouds that often cover the whole sky—like fog that doesn't reach the ground.	**Stratus:** It's probably already misting or drizzling.
White, fluffy clouds that look like cotton.	**Cumulus:** Good weather— usually.

FOG

Have you ever gotten up in the morning and looked outside—only to see cloudy whiteness covering everything? You're looking at fog.

DID YOU KNOW?
The foggiest place on Earth is the Grand Banks off the island of Newfoundland, Canada. This is where very cold water from the north meets very warm water from the south.

Fog is a giant cloud that's formed right near the ground. Different kinds of fog form for different reasons. The kind you look out your window and see is made when the ground cools overnight, bringing down the temperature of the air above it. Water vapor cools and condenses around dust and makes fog.

Another kind of fog is made when warm air moves over a cooler surface, like when warm ocean air blows over the cooler beach in the morning. The land cools down the air, creating fog. Whales love when it's foggy over the ocean. It hides them and they sing to it!

Mountains can create fog, too. When warm air slides up the side of a cool mountain, the cooled air causes fog on mountainsides. During fall and winter in California's Central Valley, a kind of fog called Tule Fog is common. Cold mountain air drops down from the Coast and Sierra Nevada Mountains. It gets stuck there for days or weeks. This fog can be so thick that sometimes you can't see farther than a foot in front of you (30 centimeters)!

3D CLOUD CHART

SUPPLIES

- ○ book or web site with cloud types and pictures
- ○ cotton
- ○ poster board
- ○ white glue
- ○ black marker with a wide tip

In this project, you'll make your own 3D cloud chart to help you remember what the different types of clouds mean.

IF YOU'RE GOING TO GO ONLINE TO LOOK FOR CLOUD PICTURES, ASK AN ADULT TO SUPERVISE.

1 Look at the chart below for the basic names and illustrations of common types of clouds. You can also look at photographs in a book or online to add other clouds, such as nimbus, altostratus, cumulonimbus, cirrocumulus, altocumulus, and stratocumulus.

2 Use the cotton to shape the different cloud types and glue them to your poster board. Label your clouds.

3 To make gray rain clouds or thunderclouds, you can gently color the cotton with the black marker.

4 Hang up your chart near a window and use it to identify the clouds you see.

CIRRUS   STRATUS   CUMULUS

65

EDIBLE CLOUDS

With this recipe, you can make edible "clouds" to share with your family and friends. Try to make them look like the different types of clouds!

HAVE AN ADULT HELP WITH THE OVEN.

SUPPLIES

○ oven

○ 4 egg whites

○ mixing bowl and electric mixer

○ $\frac{1}{2}$ teaspoon cream of tartar

○ 2 cups sugar (500 grams)

○ plastic Ziploc bag

○ scissors

○ cookie sheet

1 Preheat the oven to 200 degrees Fahrenheit (about 110 degrees Celsius—very cool).

2 Separate the egg whites into the mixing bowl. Using an electric mixer, beat the egg whites until they're foamy. Beat in the cream of tartar at medium speed. Then gradually add 2 tablespoons of sugar (31 grams).

3 When soft peaks begin to form, add another tablespoon of sugar (15 grams) and turn the mixer up to high speed. When stiff peaks form, gradually add the rest of the sugar while beating.

4 When the mixture is very stiff and shiny, you're ready to make your clouds. Spoon the mixture into your plastic Ziploc bag, and snip off one of the corners. Squeeze the bag to squirt some cloud out onto your cookie sheet in the shapes you want.

5 When you're finished creating, bake your clouds for about an hour. They should be completely dry to the touch. While you enjoy your cloud treat, explain what each one is and the weather it brings.

FOG IN A JAR

SUPPLIES

- black paper
- tape
- glass jar
- water
- food coloring
- match
- plastic Ziploc bag full of ice cubes

You can see fog form right in front of you with this project. See how thick you can "grow" your fog.

HAVE AN ADULT HELP WITH THE MATCH.

1 Tape the black paper around the back outside of the jar. This will help you see your fog better.

2 Fill the jar about a third of the way with very warm (not boiling!) water. Add a few drops of food coloring.

3 Have an adult light the match and hold it over the jar opening for a few seconds. This will warm the air in the jar and produce smoke. Then, have them toss the match into the jar. Cover the top of the jar with the bag of ice.

4 Watch inside the jar for a few minutes. You should see a little cloud of fog form. That's because the warm water begins to evaporate. The water vapor clings to the smoke particles from the match, just like they cling to dust high in the atmosphere. Then, as the air cools down from the ice, the vapor begins condensing. You've made your own fog!

67

EXTREME WEATHER

Our weather is either sunny or cloudy, or a combination of both. Sometimes it rains, or maybe it snows a little bit. No big deal, right? But then there are times when the weather can get downright crazy. There might be massive thunderstorms, a blizzard, or even a hurricane or tornado.

Extreme weather happens all over the world. However, some areas experience more extreme weather than others. For example, the middle of the United States is often called "Tornado Alley." That's because it gets more tornadoes than other parts of the country—a lot more.

THUNDERSTORMS

We all know what thunderstorms sound like, but what causes them? Thunderstorms happen when a cold air mass collides with a warm air mass. When there is a big difference in temperature between the two air masses, there is a good chance of a storm.

DID YOU KNOW?
According to some estimates, there are around 1,800 thunderstorms every day around the planet!

When the cold air mass hits the warm air mass, it rushes underneath the warm mass. That pushes the warm air mass up at a sharp angle into the atmosphere. As the warm air mass hits the higher—and colder—atmosphere, all the moisture it's carrying quickly condenses. The result is a dark storm cloud full of lightning and thunder.

Lightning is a bright flash of electricity that builds up during a thunderstorm. Think about what happens when you rub your feet on the carpet and then you touch something. Zap! You built up an electrical charge. Lightning is just like that, but on a much, much bigger scale.

Lightning is created when some of the water droplets in the storm cloud turn to ice and starting bumping into each other. As the ice particles collide and rub against each other, an electrical charge starts building up inside the cloud. At the same time, a charge is building up on the ground under the cloud. The charge is strongest around anything that sticks up—mountains, trees, even grass. The charge coming down from the cloud connects with the charge coming up from the ground—zap! You've got lightning!

WORDS TO KNOW

sound wave: invisible vibrations in the air that you hear as sound.

supercell: a severe thunderstorm with strong movements of air both up and down.

You hear thunder because the air near the lightning heats up quickly and expands. This generates a **sound wave**. It moves so fast you hear the sound we call thunder. It's like when you blow up a bag and pop it. The sound you hear is the compressed air rushing out into the space left by the flat balloon.

TORNADOES

A tornado is nature's most violent storm. Everyone knows the familiar "twister" shape of a tornado. These spinning columns of air start from powerful thunderstorms called **supercells** that go all the way down to the ground. The strongest tornado winds swirl up to 300 miles per hour (480 kilometers per hour), destroying large buildings and trees in seconds.

EXTREME WEATHER

Most tornadoes last only five or ten minutes, but some have been known to last more than an hour. Some tornadoes are relatively weak and some are very strong. The strength of tornadoes can be measured on the Enhanced Fujita scale.

ENHANCED FUJITA SCALE LEVEL AND WIND SPEED	WHAT CAN HAPPEN . . .
EF0/65–85 MPH (105–137 KPH)	Tree branches break, and there is some roof damage.
EF1/86–110 MPH (138–177 KPH)	Roofs start coming off, and moving cars can be pushed off roads.
EF2/111–135 MPH (178–217 KPH)	There is a lot of damage. Mobile homes are destroyed, train cars are pushed over, and large trees can be uprooted.
EF3/136–165 MPH (218–266 KPH)	Roofs and walls are torn off.
EF4/166–200 MPH (267–322 KPH)	Houses are destroyed and cars can be thrown.
EF5/201+ MPH (322+ KPH)	Homes are lifted up, carried a great distance, and completely destroyed. Cars are thrown through the air great distances, and concrete and steel structures are badly damaged.

Have you ever seen a tornado? There are close to 1,000 tornadoes in the United States every year. This is more than anywhere else in the world. Most of these storms happen in Tornado Alley between Texas and South Dakota.

In the spring and summer, warm, wet air from the Gulf of Mexico rises up to meet cool, dry air coming down from Canada. The Canadian winds higher up in the atmosphere blow at a different speed than Gulf winds lower down. When they collide, they can create a spinning storm.

If the winds are lined up just right and are strong enough, the storm spins like a top and makes a funnel cloud. When rain and hail fall from the storm, the funnel drops until it touches ground. It's time to take shelter because a tornado has landed!

HURRICANES

Hurricanes are massive tropical storms that form over warm ocean water. The warm, moist air rises upward, and air from the surrounding area swirls into the space left by the rising air. Then that air is warmed when it comes into contact with the ocean and it too rises up. The cycle continues, growing into a powerful, spiraling windstorm.

As the storm begins to spin faster and faster, an "eye" forms in the very center. The eye is calm and clear. People who experience the eye of a hurricane often think the hurricane is over—but there's a whole second part to come! Hurricanes don't stay together very well once they hit land. But their heavy rains, strong winds, and large waves can do a lot of damage to buildings, trees, and cars in coastal areas.

DID YOU KNOW?

Hurricane *Katrina* devastated New Orleans, Louisiana, in August 2005. It was the third deadliest hurricane in United States history, with 1,836 people dead from the storm and hundreds still missing.

THIS IS A SEVERE WEATHER WARNING...

Like tornadoes, there's a scale to measure how big hurricanes are. It's called the Saffir-Simpson Hurricane Scale.

SAFFIR-SIMPSON SCALE LEVEL AND WIND SPEED	WHAT CAN HAPPEN . . .
CATEGORY 1 74–95 MPH (119–153 KPH)	Mobile homes are toppled over, trees snap, and there is coastal flooding, and pier damage.
CATEGORY 2 96–110 MPH (154–177 KPH)	Houses can be lifted, mobile homes damaged, and trees can suffer a lot of damage.
CATEGORY 3 111–130 MPH (178–209 KPH)	This is a major hurricane. Damage to buildings is severe, mobile homes are destroyed, and there is a lot of flooding along the coast and a bit inland.
CATEGORY 4 131–155 MPH (210–249 KPH)	Many homes are completely destroyed, and flooding can happen far inland.
CATEGORY 5 OVER 156 MPH (OVER 250 KPH)	Buildings are completely destroyed, there is major flooding far inland, and total destruction affects much of the area.

EXTREME WEATHER

| CATEGORY 1 | CATEGORY 2 | CATEGORY 3 | CATEGORY 4 | CATEGORY 5 |

DID YOU KNOW?

There are people called hurricane hunters. They fly sturdy planes right up to and into the hurricane to take measurements and report back about the conditions.

Unlike tornadoes, hurricanes can last for a while. To keep track of them, hurricanes are given names. The names go in alphabetical order, alternating between boy and girl names. At the beginning of each hurricane season, names restart again from the letter A. If a storm turns out to be devastating or deadly, that name is never used again. Each season there are about five or six named hurricanes. The official hurricane season is from June 1 to November 30, when most, but not all, hurricanes happen.

LIGHTNING: Part One

You can't make real lightning, of course, but this activity will show you how everything carries an electrical charge. You'll be able to see how lightning really does happen.

SUPPLIES

- ○ disposable foil pie pan
- ○ pencil with full eraser
- ○ tack
- ○ foam plate
- ○ piece of wool fabric

1 Turn the foil pie pan upside down. Hold the pencil on the pan with the eraser down. Push the tack through the center of the pie pan from underneath into the eraser.

2 Put the foam plate upside down on a table, and rub the bottom with wool fabric quickly for a few minutes. Try not to handle the plate.

3 Pick up the foil pie pan using the pencil as a handle. Place it on top of the foam plate. Then, touch the pie pan with your finger. You should feel a small shock! If not, rub the foam plate again, but longer. If you do this in the dark, you'll even see a little spark.

4 Just like with real lightning, it's all about the charges of electricity. The charges on the pie pan come from the wool-rubbed foam plate. They jump to the charges on your finger, just like a teeny tiny lightning bolt.

ZAP!

LIGHTNING: Part Two

Have you ever seen lightning in your mouth? In this activity you will . . . don't worry, this activity is harmless and tasty!

SUPPLIES

- dark room
- wintergreen or peppermint Lifesavers candy
- mirror

1 Turn off the lights and wait a few minutes while your eyes get used to the dark. Then, pop a couple of candies into your mouth.

2 Keep your mouth open as much as you can, and watch yourself in the mirror as you crunch down on the candies. You should see sparks flying right in your mouth!

CHOMP
CHOMP

3 In this experiment, you're releasing the little electrical charges inside the sugar. They're reacting to the opposite charges right in your mouth, creating tiny bursts of electrical current.

THUNDERSNOW

Thunder in winter? You don't usually hear thunder in winter, but there can be lightning in a heavy snowstorm. And when there's lightning, there's thunder! This is called thundersnow. Thundersnow can only happen if there's a lot of moisture in the air. Most thundersnow happens near large lakes, such as the Great Salt Lake in Utah or any of the Great Lakes along the border of the United States and Canada.

WEATHER STATION

In this project, you'll make your own weather station using some of the other projects in this book. You'll be able to check your weather instruments every day and write down what you observe. You can even try to predict the weather for the next day, and then see how accurate you are!

SUPPLIES

- ☼ 2 thick dowels, at least 1½ feet long (about 48 centimeters)
- ☼ pegboard
- ☼ pipe cleaners
- ☼ some of the other projects in this book, like the windsock, barometer, anemometer, and rain gauge
- ☼ clipboard with paper
- ☼ pencil

1 Attach the dowels to the back of the pegboard using pipe cleaners, twisting them tightly. Let the dowels extend about a foot past the base of the pegboard (30 centimeters). You'll use these to stick the weather station into the ground.

2 Using the pegboard as a base, attach the weather instruments (the other projects you've made from this book) with the pipe cleaners. You can attach the windsock onto a top corner and the anemometer onto the other corner so they don't block each other.

3 Make sure nothing is blocking anything else. You want your barometer straw to move freely, for example. And you want the rain gauge to have a clear opening to the sky.

4 Set your weather station outside where it won't get bumped. Push the dowels into the ground so the weather station is upright and stable. Check your weather instruments every day to make sure everything is working properly.

5 Make a chart on the paper and clip it to the clipboard. Columns should include: Day, Observation, Prediction, and Actual Weather. Record your observations each day.

MCMURDO STATION

There is a weather station in Antarctica that people actually live in. It's called McMurdo Station and it is Antarctica's largest community. Most people at McMurdo are scientists from the United States Antarctic Program. Over 1,000 people live at McMurdo in the summer and about 200 people in winter. But the seasons at McMurdo are only cold and colder. Or light and dark. "Summer" is the four months when it is light all day, while "winter" is the four months when it is always dark. During the other months, the sun is coming or going. And average temperatures are always below freezing!

WEATHER SAFETY KIT

You can't stop bad weather from happening. But you can be prepared for it. Keep your family safe by having this weather safety kit always stocked and ready for anything that comes your way. Keep a weather safety kit in your car, too.

SUPPLIES

- ☼ paper and pen
- ☼ a big, sturdy plastic box with a lid
- ☼ tape
- ☼ assorted emergency items (see step 1 for suggestions)

1 Talk with your family about what should be put into the weather safety kit. Some ideas include: food and water, blankets, a first-aid kit, flashlights and batteries, a multifunction tool, waterproof matches, plastic bags, tissues or toilet paper, and a battery-powered radio. Energy bars and dried fruit are good food choices because they last a long time. Write down your list. Then, gather everything together and put it in the box.

2 Write down emergency phone numbers on the paper—such as the electric company, police, fire, as well as friends and family.

3 Tape the list to the inside of the lid. This way, if you use anything up, you can use it as a checklist to know what to replace.

4 Store your weather safety kit in a place where you can get to it easily in case of a storm, like in a hall closet. You want to be able to locate the box easily in the dark.

TORNADO IN A BOTTLE

You can get an idea about how a tornado looks—without having to go chase one down yourself!

SUPPLIES

- empty 2-liter plastic bottle with cap
- water
- liquid soap
- vinegar
- glitter and food coloring

1 Remove any labels and clean the empty plastic bottle, if necessary. Fill the bottle about three-quarters full with water.

2 Add about a teaspoon each of the liquid soap and the vinegar (5 milliliters). Add glitter and food coloring.

3 Screw on the cap tightly and shake the bottle to mix the ingredients.

4 Now hold the bottle upside down and swirl it in a circular motion. A funnel-shaped whirlpool will form inside. You've got your own small tornado!

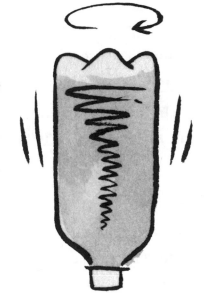

CLIMATE CHANGE

Daily forecasts may not be perfect, but you can always have a general idea of what to expect when you step outside. If you live in the United States and in the north, you know it's going to be cold in the winter. Ponds freeze and it usually snows. Ice skating and sledding are more likely activities than riding your bicycle. And if you're down south in the summer, you expect it to be steaming hot. A swim and a cold glass of lemonade are what you want!

You know this because the climate of an area is pretty steady each year. The temperature ranges of each season are fairly predictable. But what if you look at the big picture—the climate of an area over a huge amount of time, not just one year or even ten years?

CLIMATE CHANGE

If you were to make a giant chart that tracked the weather over hundreds and thousands of years, you might find that the climate of an area varied over time. It might have been colder during the Ice Age around 20,000 years ago. Or it might have been warmer 1,000 years ago, when Earth's climate was wetter and warmer than it is today.

Unlike daily changes in weather, climate changes are very, very slow. It's not like you'd walk out the door one day and be sweating, and the very next day need a coat and mittens. The change takes place so slowly that scientists have to look back at large periods of time to see **trends**.

WORDS TO KNOW

trend: movement toward something.

crop: plants grown for food and other uses.

livestock: animals raised for food and other products.

IS IT CHILLY IN HERE?

One example of climate change was the "Little Ice Age" from about 1550 to 1850. While it wasn't as dramatic an event as the Ice Age when huge glaciers dominated most of the earth, it still had a big impact on the people who lived during that time. Existing glaciers expanded, creeping over farmland. Rivers and canals froze. Snowfall was much higher than normal. **Crops** failed and **livestock** died, leaving people starving and struggling.

WHAT'S GOING ON?

Scientists think there are different reasons for changes in climate. It could be the result of tiny changes in Earth's orbit or its tilt toward the sun. Sometimes the sun's output of heat changes just a bit. You wouldn't notice these events, but the climate would change ever so slightly.

Another cause can be strong eruptions of volcanoes. These can shoot very fine dust high in the atmosphere. The dust particles can weaken the strength of sunlight for months. And that's enough to affect the climate for a period of time.

GLOBAL WARMING

There's another cause of climate change: human activity here on Earth. Many scientists understand that global temperatures are increasing because of how humans live their lives today. When

people burn **fossil fuels** like natural gas, oil, and coal for their energy needs, like heating their homes or driving their cars, they release gases into the atmosphere. Those gases, including carbon dioxide, form an invisible blanket around the planet. This blanket keeps heat trapped close to Earth—and the temperature all over the globe is rising very slowly. This is called **global warming**.

CLIMATE CHANGE

WORDS TO KNOW

fossil fuel: three forms of fuel that we can burn for energy—oil, natural gas, and coal. It formed over 300 million years ago from tiny fossils of plants and animals. When we use it up, fossil fuels will be gone forever.

global warming: an increase in the average temperature of the earth's atmosphere.

greenhouse gas: a gas in the atmosphere that traps heat.

The gases themselves are called **greenhouse gases**, because they act just like the glass of a greenhouse. They let sunlight in to warm the earth, but stop heat from escaping.

Rising global temperatures means less rain and more drought. It also means that glaciers are melting, which causes the levels of the world's oceans to rise. All these changes put animals, plants, and people at risk.

DID YOU KNOW?

20 million tons of ice are being lost every day by just one of the glaciers in Greenland. This is equal to the amount of water used by the entire population of New York City in a full year!

The earth only has a certain amount of natural gas, oil, and coal to begin with. Scientists and concerned people are asking everyone to use less of these fossil fuels too. If you recycle your trash and reuse what you have, you can save fossil fuels. Not only will this preserve what the planet has, but it will also reduce the amount of greenhouse gases going into the atmosphere. By slowing global warming, the planet can experience its own natural climate changes over long periods of time.

GLOBAL WARMING CHECKLIST

There's a lot we can all do to help pitch in and cut back on the use of fossil fuels. Make this checklist for your family so you'll know how you can help.

SUPPLIES

- colorful paper
- markers
- clear sheet protector
- dry erase marker
- string
- tape

1 Using the starter list below, write each item on its own line and make a big box beside it.

2 Keep adding to the list until you've thought of as many ways as possible. When you've finished, slip your list inside the sheet protector.

3 Tie a string around the dry erase marker, and tape the end to the sheet protector.

4 Hang your list where everyone in the family can easily see it every day—like the refrigerator.

5 Each day, encourage your family to check off on the outside of the sheet protector what they've done to help protect the environment. At the end of the day, erase the marks and start fresh the next day.

adapt: to change in order to survive.

air mass: a large pocket of air that is different from the air around it.

air pressure: the force of the gases surrounding the earth pressing downward (sometimes called barometric pressure).

altitude: the height of something above the level of the sea. Also called elevation.

anemometer: a weather instrument that measures wind speed.

atmosphere: the gases surrounding the earth.

barometer: a weather instrument that measures air pressure.

barometric pressure: the force of the atmosphere pressing downward (also called air pressure).

canopy: up in the trees of the rainforest.

climate: the average weather in an area over a long period of time.

climate zone: a large region with a similar climate.

condense: when water vapor turns into liquid water.

contract: to shrink and take up less space.

crop: plants grown for food and other uses.

decade: a 10-year period.

dense: when molecules are pressed tightly together.

digital: when a device shows information as numbers.

drought: a long period of time when there is too little rain.

ecosystem: the plants and animals that make up an environment.

environment: the area in which something lives.

equator: an invisible line dividing the earth into the Northern and Southern Hemispheres.

evaporate: when a liquid turns into a gas.

expand: to spread out and take up more space.

flood: when water covers an area that is usually dry.

food chain: plants and animals in an environment where each is eaten by another higher up in the chain.

fossil fuel: three forms of fuel that we can burn for energy—oil, natural gas, and coal. It formed over 300 million years ago from tiny fossils of plants and animals. When we use it up, fossil fuels will be gone forever.

GLOSSARY

glacier: a huge mass of ice and snow.

global warming: an increase in the average temperature of the earth's atmosphere.

gravity: a force that pulls objects to the earth.

greenhouse gas: a gas in the atmosphere that traps heat.

heat index: the air temperature combined with the humidity in the air.

heat stroke: a condition when your body gets dangerously overheated.

humidity: a high amount of moisture in the air.

hurricane: a bad storm with high winds.

leeward side: the side that doesn't get hit by the traveling winds.

livestock: animals raised for food and other products.

mercury: a liquid metal used inside thermometers.

meteorologist: a person who studies the science of weather and climate.

mild: not too hot and not too cold.

molecule: a group of the tiniest particles.

monsoon: a wind that brings heavy rainfall to southern Asia in summer.

Northern Hemisphere: the half of the earth north of the equator. The southern half is called the Southern Hemisphere.

observation: something you observe.

observe: to look at things carefully.

orbit: the path a planet takes around the sun.

polar: the cold climate zones near the North and South Poles.

precipitation: water in the air in any form, like snow, hail, or rain, that falls to the ground.

prediction: something you predict.

predict: to say what will happen in the future.

radar: a system that sends out pulses of radio waves that reflect back.

rain shadow: an area beside a mountain that gets little or no rain because it all fell on the mountain itself.

recycle: to use something again.

region: a large area of the earth.

scale: a measuring system.

sound wave: invisible vibrations in the air that you hear as sound.

Southern Hemisphere: the half of the earth south of the equator.

species: a group of plants or animals that are related and look the same.

sphere: round, like a ball.

supercell: a severe thunderstorm with strong movements of air both up and down.

technology: tools, methods, and systems used to solve a problem or do work.

temperate: the moderate climate zones between the tropical and polar regions.

temperature: how warm or cold something is.

thermometer: a weather instrument used to measure temperature.

tornado: a violent, twisting column of air.

trend: movement toward something.

tropical: the hot climate zone to the north and south of the equator.

water cycle: the natural recycling of water.

water vapor: the gas form of water when it's evaporated in the air.

weather forecast: to say what the weather will be.

weather instrument: a tool that measures wind, temperature, or something else about the weather.

weather pattern: repeating weather over a number of days or weeks.

weather satellite: a small electronic object that circles the earth and sends back pictures of weather patterns.

weather: what it's like outside—warm, cold, sunny, cloudy, rainy, snowy, or windy.

wind chill: what the combination of air temperature and wind feels like on your skin.

windward side: the side that faces into the oncoming winds.

RESOURCES

BOOKS

Breen, Mark, and Kathleen Friestad.
Kids' Book of Weather Forecasting. Ideals, 2008

Cole, Joanna. *The Magic School Bus Inside A Hurricane*.
Scholastic Press, 1996

Fradin, Judy, and Dennis. *Tornado! The Story Behind These
Twisting, Turning, Spinning, and Spiraling Storms*.
National Geographic Children's Books, 2011

Furgang, Kathy. *National Geographic Kids Everything Weather:
Facts, Photos, and Fun that Will Blow You Away*.
National Geographic Children's Books, 2012

Larson, Kirby, and Mary Nethery. *Two Bobbies: A True Story of Hurricane
Katrina, Friendship, and Survival*. Walker Children's, 2008

WEB SITES

Weather Channel Kids, theweatherchannelkids.com
Get your forecast, watch videos, and explore a weather dictionary.

FEMA for Kids, ready.gov/kids/home.html
*Games, facts, and fun stuff to help keep you and your family
safe during a weather emergency.*

NOAA for Kids, oceanservice.noaa.gov/kids
Explore the oceans and skies and see how they affect your weather.

HowStuffWorks, science.howstuffworks.com/nature/climate-weather
Interesting tidbits about weather.

Weather Wiz Kids, weatherwizkids.com
Info on different weather events.

INDEX